JUST JOSHIN' YA

Foreword

Joy is everlasting happiness. If you know anything about joy, you know it feels like a ray of sunshine wherever you go, whatever situation you're in. Joy Anna knows how to take any experience in life and turn it into a blessing and a learning experience, and she usually adds a touch of humor along the way. Much like a hummingbird is graceful, peaceful, mesmerizing, and unpredictable, Joy Anna always finds the sweet nectar of life.

What do you need to know about the author?
She is Joy.

— JILL GARNER -

JUST JOSHIN' YA

JOY ANNA

Copyright © 2019 by Joyanna "Joy" Diaz

Published by JoyEl Publishing

Percentage of the proceeds of this book are donated to individuals affected by cancer.

Edit and Formatting services provided by Stacey Smekofske EditsByStacey.com

Cover Design by amazing anonymous

ISBN: 978-1-952123-00-9 paperback

978-1-952123-01-6 digital book

All rights reserved.

No part of this book may be reproduced in any form or by any electronic or mechanical means, including information storage and retrieval systems, without written permission from the author, except for the use of brief quotations in a book review.

This Book is dedicated to Brandon, Danielle and Joshua.

*On Sunday 8/31/08, I wrote the following excerpt in my journal: My Joshua, I was reading a book today that contained the saying, "The perfect ones can be taken home
early." I pray God will let me keep you forever. You are my joy, you are my son, such a joy. I am blessed God allowed me to nurture, raise and teach you.*

I am thankful, grateful and blessed beyond measure for my kids Brandon, Danielle and Joshua. I had someone tell me that you cannot love a stepchild and an adopted child as much as your natural child and that it is not the truth. I love all three of you with the same dedication. I love you just as you are and for who you are. I am so proud of all of you.

"A joyful heart is good medicine."

— PROVERBS 17:22 NAS

CONTENTS

Introduction	xiii
JOSH SPEAK	
Random Joshing	3
You've Been Joshed	23
JOSHIN AROUND	
Joshisms	33
Joshastrations	35
About the Author	43
Also by Joy Anna	45
Letter to the Reader	47

Introduction

In 2008, my BFF Shari bought a journal for my 41st birthday. "Joy Journal" was printed on the cover, but my life was far from joyous at that time. My teenage daughter despised me, my husband was always angry at me, and between the two of them, every day was a fight to survive.

While driving and juggling my hectic mom-work role, I found myself laughing out loud at a conversation with my 4-year-old son. In that moment, I experienced an epiphany. I should be writing these moments of joy in my journal. While I admit I didn't capture even a third of these moments, I did start writing them down.

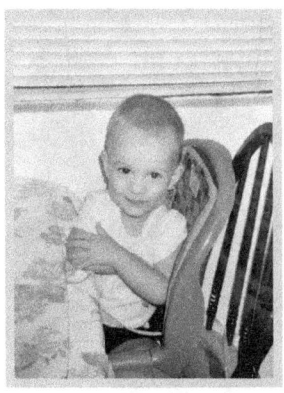

In 2015 I found myself sitting alone at Hope Cancer Clinic, waiting for chemotherapy after my double mastectomy. I

INTRODUCTION

picked up a small, square, glossy-covered book in the waiting area. As I read each page, I felt my cheeks lift. I needed to smile, and I decided I had to publish my joy journal somehow, someway. After ten surgeries and the urging of many close friends in my life, I found my excellent editor, Stacey, and the rest is history. These preserved words lifted my spirits in some of my lowest times. My hope that is that while reading these words that you too will feel your cheeks lift with a smile and feel JOY.

#SharedStoriesChangeLives

Grateful, Thankful and Joyous,

Joy Anna

JOSH SPEAK

Random Joshing

Joshua was eating dinner and out of the blue announced, "I am so stuffed I should be called a turkey!"

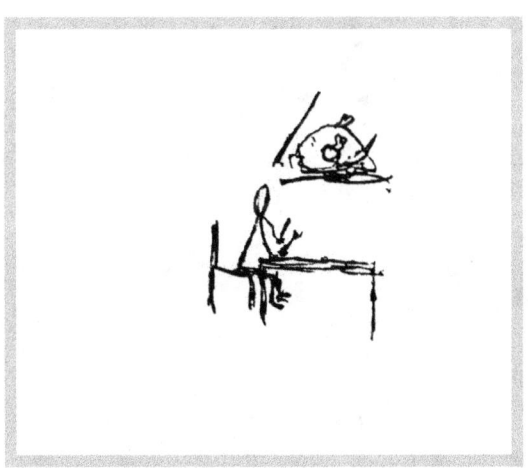

Joshua has been having difficulty remembering to zip his fly- not a big deal, but I am having to remind him almost daily. Today he got up, dressed himself in red, net type sport shorts and a white long-sleeved tee shirt. A few hours into our day he says, "Well mom, it's a good thing I picked out these sport shorts today, so I don't have to worry about zipping my fly today!"

Joshua dressed up to go out for a really nice dinner. He was told, "Hey buddy you look really sharp!" Joshua looked up confused and leaned over to me saying, "I'm not pokey- I'm soft all over!"

A very tired Joshua piped up from his car seat, "My brain is so tired it went to La La Land."

I asked Joshua a question, and he replied, "Is that a permanent question?" He meant to say, "Is that a rhetorical question". *He is trying to use big words when he talks.*

Joshua was so wiggly in his car seat today. I looked up in the rear-view mirror and asked him if he was ok. He said, "I have an itchy butt." I said "ewwwwww." He yells, "MOOOOOM; in the soft part, NOT the icky part!"

While Joshua ate a hot dog, he was observed to be holding it too tight. "Don't hold it so tight, you'll squish it." Joshua replied, "I am not holding it like Death Valley." *He meant to say death grip.*

It was book fair time at school and taxes were due the next day. Joshua said, "Mom, don't you think you should buy me a book before you give all your money to the government?"

. . .

We attended a large playdate pool party at a friend's house. After it was all over, we drove home. Joshua asked about an older friend that still had to wear arm floaties to swim. I answered him that not everyone is blessed to have a pool like we did so that we could practice swimming. I told him not everyone has the ability to swim or has learned how to swim. I hear silence for a brief moment and then he pipes up, "Oh! You mean like in Africa they do others things like shoot turkeys, kill hyenas and build Indian homes."

One day, I took Joshua to Einstein bagels. The employee behind the counter asked Joshua what kind of bagel he wanted. Joshua replied, "Just plain." Then the employee asked him if he wanted the plain bagel with cream cheese and toasted. Joshua replied, "Just cream cheese please." While we watched the employees work to prepare our order, Joshua turned to me and whispered, "I hope they don't mess up my order, I don't like roasted bagels." I corrected Joshua and said, "Honey it's toasted not roasted." He said, "No Mom. Toast get toasted, not bagels."

Joshua said, "I'm so tired, I am brain-washed—you know just like the washing machine? That's what my head feels like...the spin cycle."

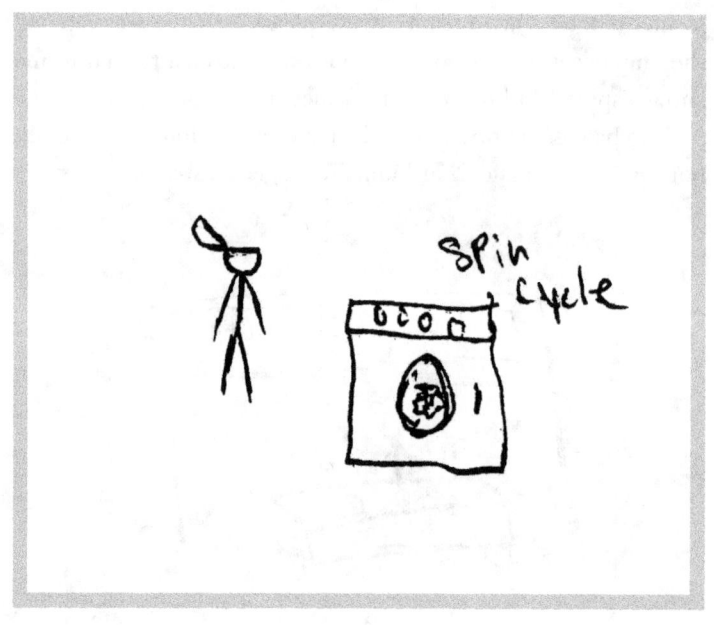

JUST JOSHIN' YA

While on vacation in Hawaii, Joshua overheard one of the locals warn us about the torrential rains that cause pools of water. The local said that after standing for a while, the pool will be full of *bacteria*. The next morning on the beach Joshua chatted with a new beach friend in the sand telling them all about the, "Vacteria. Vacteria in the standing water--the dangerous vacteria."

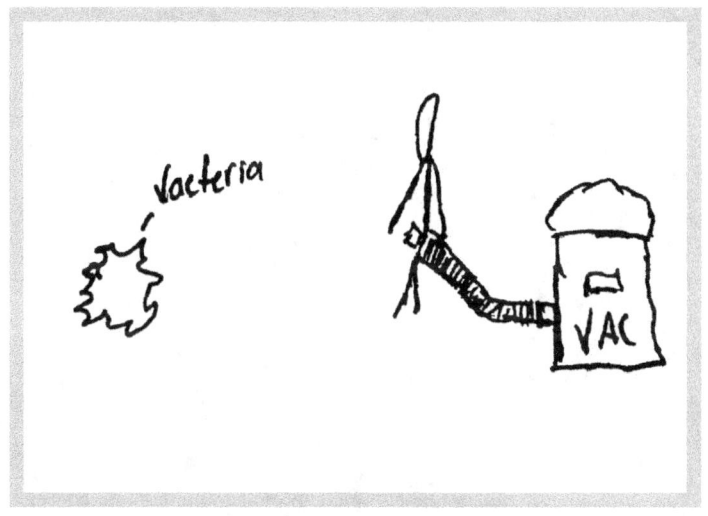

JOY ANNA

On our way to San Diego to see the Padres play, Joshua piped up from the back seat and asked if we were in Victory-ville yet. *It's pronounced Victorville, CA.*

For the second year in a row, we drove to Magic Mountain in CA for a special event. Joshua spoke up from the back seat and said, "My head is trying to have a BIG MEMORY from a long time ago about this place!"

We stayed up tonight to watch a movie until 9:15 pm which was very late for Joshua. After the movie, he sat up and said, "I'm as tired as a sheep, a dead sheep."

The roosters in Kauai, Hawaii are infamously known as friggin' chickens because they squawk and crow at 4 am. The first morning they slept in Joshua ran into the room announcing, "MOM! The chickens didn't turn on until 6 o'clock this morning!"

Joshua was looking in my wallet and spied my driver's license. He saw the F under sex and said, "Wow mom you flunked sex? Is it because you didn't take it, or did you forget to study?"

When Joshua was four years old, he said out loud in the back seat, "I need to educate myself correctly, so I will get a good job, so I can make money and travel the world."

I was at a cat show with our cat, Zorro. I was trying to get him qualified to be a Grand National Winner. I entered Joshua's cat, Rocky in the same show, but Rocky was not pulling purple winner ribbons. It was ok because I didn't expect him to win. Joshua got upset because his cat wasn't getting ribbons. I did my best to explain that it was ok, that I didn't expect Rocky to win. I said he was sort of a lame duck in the group. Later on, I heard Joshua telling a friend, "I have such a lame cat because he didn't win any ribbons."

One Christmas, Joshua came with me to the Holiday Ice Show featuring Michael W. Smith, Amy Smith and famous ice skaters like Nancy Kerrigan. I was driving and listening to Michael W. Smith when Joshua asked me, "Mom is this Michael W. Smith." I said yes, and Joshua says, "Are there people ice skating around him while he plays the piano and sings?" That one took me awhile to connect the two, but I finally did.

While I was putting Joshua to bed he asked in a sleepy voice, "Mom, where does your spit come from? Cause I keep swallowing it down my throat, and it keeps coming back to my mouth."

While I was in the middle of a conference call, Joshua asked me if he could have one of the big pages of my notepad. Because I was in the middle of sketching and diagraming, I handed him a smaller post-it sized piece of paper. This is the art he drew for me.

JUST JOSHIN' YA

Joshua had been complaining that he is like an only child since his step brother and adopted sister are so much older than he is. He asked me if he could have a brother or sister. I told him that it was not physically possible for my body to have any more babies. Later, he brought the subject up again at dinner. I patiently explained that I can't have any more babies. He replied, "How do you know? Doesn't your tummy tell you if you're having another baby?"

Joshua groaned when I picked him up from a play date and said his legs were sore from doing lounges with his legs. Instead of *lunges*.

Joshua and I walked, holding hands. I asked him if he would always hold my hand, even when I'm old? He said, "No! When you're old, I will carry you."

We watched the movie *Soul Surfer* with Bethany Hamilton and we mentioned it would be nice to move to Kauai. Joshua said, "I wouldn't move there because of all the natural disasters."

"What disasters Joshua?"

He replied, "Hurricanes, earthquake, tsunamis, and chicken disease!" Oh, the famous friggin' chickens.

I served Joshua scrambled eggs, and just like his older brother he liked to slather them in red sauce. However, Joshua preferred spicy sauce. "Mom. Can I have some Tobacco sauce please?" Instead of *Tabasco Sauce*.

Spending time with his cousins in Colorado, Joshua had a lot to learn about getting along with others and communicating with kids. They were all playing baseball and using a Barbie doll bat. Being true cousins, they started to tease him, and they would not throw him the ball. So, he got irritated and yelled, "You better throw me the ball or I am gonna hit you with my woman stick!" The cousins laughed even harder which didn't help things.

Joshua was with his cousins swimming and they kept busy by throwing coins and rocks into the pool and diving to collect them. Shane said, "Joshua, I will hold the loot for you." Joshua said, "No, thank you. I have a pocket." Shane asked, "Where? You have a swimsuit on." Joshua got out of the pool and showed Shane his *pocket* in his underwear.

It was a tough morning. I was yapping at Joshua nonstop to get it in gear, gather his things for the day, and get in the truck. I was frustrated and trying to get to the office. When we finally loaded up, I turned to him and said, "Mommy loves you even when she's cross." Joshua says, "MOOOOOOOOOOm! No one uses that word anymore. Use REAL words like, angry, mad, and upset. Only Sir Tumpum (from Thomas the tank engine) uses the word cross."

Out from the kitchen a voice yelled, "How do you spell mister?" Joshua yelled back, "Capital M period. Capital R period."

. . .

JUST JOSHIN' YA

Joshua was working on spelling words and kept saying the word, "*Sign-a-go-jew* out loud." I said, "Joshua, what word are you trying to pronounce and spell?" He repeated out loud, "*Sign-a-go-jew*." After rolling it around in my head, I finally figured it out. Joshua was using phonics to spell *synagogue!*

While watching the battleship movie, music from AC/DC played. Joshua said, "Hey mom. What's up with these screaming dudes?"

When I was busy trying to finish my degree, Joshua, and I talked about college and the types of degrees people get. The next day Joshua stated, "I am going to get my physical degree because I play baseball."

We were watching a Food Network show featuring the grand opening of a brand new famous chef's restaurant. Many famous people showed up to the grand opening, and then Martha Stewart arrived. Joshua saw the announcement and said, "Oh Martha Stewart, she must be married to the car guy Tony Stewart!"

Joshua once said, "No mom. *Sons of Guns* is not a bad TV show. They bleep on all the bad words."

Joshua was in the bathroom for a long time. I asked him if he was ok. He yelled, "My butt is on fire!" I asked, "Why?" He yelled back, "Because of Mexican food and a cheap pepperoni stick from 7-11!"

JUST JOSHIN' YA

We were driving after school on the strip in old town Las Vegas. Joshua saw a wedding party celebrating at a drive through wedding chapel. He said, "You don't get married in a fake church, on the strip, in the hood."

JOY ANNA

While we were reminiscing about a family member's wedding, Joshua asked about the symbolic pillow with the rings that he got to carry. I explained that the maid of honor and the best man carry the real rings. Joshua responded, "Boy did I get gipped. I didn't get to do my whole job, AND I was thinking that Brandon and Lindsey couldn't afford very good rings since they were plastic."

Joshua was asked to give a company example at school. The teacher just needed a name. Joshua responded by choosing the company named Ahem Rentals. The teacher questioned Joshua about it being a real company. Joshua responded, "Oh yes! They are the company that rent all the big yellow construction stuff we see on the corner on the way to my baseball practices." I laughed when he repeated the story to me, and I told him that the company is called *Ahern Rentals*.

Joshua's legs were hurting and aching and he came to me complaining. I told him he must be growing. "Yes," he responded, "I am having HURTEVERYTHING-ITUS." I laughed and then he said, "Actually mom, I am having a growth sprout." *Instead of growth spurt!*

You've Been Joshed

Joshua's nighttime ritual is to watch either *How It's Made*, *Dirty Jobs*, or the Weather Channel or Food TV. One night, while watching Food TV, Rachel Ray came on to give tips about visiting Martha's Vineyard and share yummy recipes from that region. At the end of the show, Rachel came back on and said, "Thanks for watching, and I hope you all enjoyed all of our tips. We loved sharing them with you!" Joshua turned to me and said, "Mom do you have any tips you want to share with Food TV?"

One of the key phrases my mom used her entire life was, "For crying out loud." For example: For crying out loud, Joy. Why didn't you finish washing all the dishes? Or for crying out loud, can you believe they ran out of sweet tea? I could tell that the kids were getting frustrated with each other and then I heard Joshua say, "For crying sake, Sissy. Stop bugging me."

. . .

We were driving on the 215 freeway where they were doing extensive road construction. They erected a huge pile of dirt in the middle of the mess and have a large America flag stuck in the top of the huge dirt pile. My daughter comments out loud, "Why did they put that big American flag up there?" Joshua pipes up and answers, "Silly sister, because it's the grave of an American president."

JUST JOSHIN' YA

We stopped at a chain restaurant for lunch while visiting in Utah. Joshua came out of the bathroom and asked me, "How did they get diesel in the bathroom?" I responded, "What?" Joshua said, "Yeah, there is a sign hanging in the bathroom that says, 'Employees must wash their hands to stop the spread of diesel.'" I visited the ladies' room, hoping I can figure out what he was talking about. There was the sign, "Employees must wash their hands to stop the spread of *disease*."

One day, Joshua had to stay home from school due an allergic reaction. So I had no choice but to take him with me on a busy workday. We had many stops and many interruptions. At lunch, he told me, "Today didn't han out like it was supposed to." I said Joshua, "It's *pan* out." And he says, "Well, that doesn't make sense. How do pans get out?"

On the way out of town for a wedding, we stopped to eat pizza and packed up the leftovers to eat later on the plane. Joshua was worried that the pizza wouldn't taste very good cold. I told him I used to eat leftover cold pizza when I was little. Joshua asked, "Why? Because they didn't make microwaves back then?"

While cooking in the kitchen the song "Our House" by Madness came on. I started to sing and dance to it, "Our house, in the middle of the street." Joshua came around the corner and said, "WOW- you know the words to THAT song? I thought that song was waaaaay old, from the 70s."

While reviewing Joshua's homework, he told me he needed to study for a bible verse quiz. I asked him what translation his teacher used, KJV (King James Version) or NIV (New International Version). He paused and said, "Holy."

Cousin Shane was carrying Joshua around on his back in the pool like a sea horse. Joshua got off and said, "Thanks, Shane. You remind me of Michael Phillips." Instead of *Michael Phelps* the famous Olympian swimmer.

Joshua asked about getting baptized, so I contacted our Pastor Matt who graciously and patiently explained what baptism was all about. One of the questions that Pastor Matt asked Joshua was, "Do you remember when Jesus died on the cross?" Joshua responded, "Well, I didn't actually see it, but I read about it in the Bible."

Granny Jo and Poppa were watching the US Open with Joshua. It was an exciting tie breaker match involving Roger Federer. Poppa yelled out from the kitchen, "Who is ahead?" Granny Jo answered, "I think Federer is serving to tie it." Joshua added, "Oh his last name is tie- it?"

Joshua had a homework assignment to write a sentence, "All about your family." I looked over his shoulder and saw he had started a sentence, "Danielle picks on me and doesn't tell the truth and is..." I stopped him and said, "Hey wait a minute. You don't need to write negative stuff like that for school." He replied, "Well she is." So, I said, "Joshua, write something positive like, 'Sissy plays games.'" He interrupted me and said, "No, she doesn't like to." I said, "Ok what about, 'Sissy taught me DS.'" He said, "No she didn't." I gave several examples to which Joshua replied, "No, no, no. Mom she didn't." I finally said, "Joshua, you need to be positive. We don't speak negatively to others about our family in public. So you need to come up with something positive." The following morning, I looked at the homework page, smudged from much erasing, and it said, "I HAVE A SISTER NAMED DANIELLE."

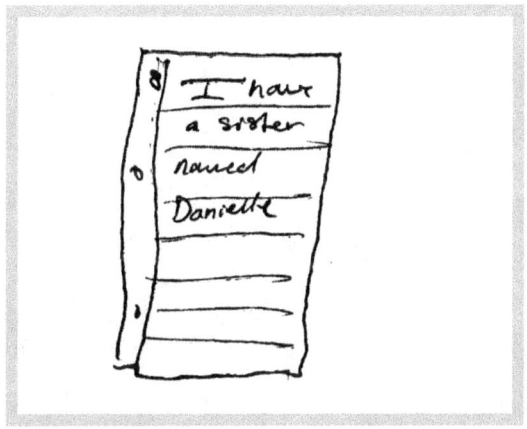

JOSHIN AROUND

Joshisms

"It's mighty wrong to be wearing a thong when you're writing a song."

Joshua yelled out when he saw an ice cream billboard, "It's totally the dream of my life!"

"This tastes like body odor smells."

"That white one tastes like what Coppertone sunscreen smells like." *Coconut*

Saying "Constipation" instead of *Condensation/Evaporation*.

. . .

After leaving a glass of water out in the sun for a couple of hours and seeing that the water had evaporated Joshua yelled out, "I LOVE SCIENCE!"

"How does a missile float, like what's its fire power?"

Joshastrations

JOY ANNA

JUST JOSHIN' YA

JOY ANNA

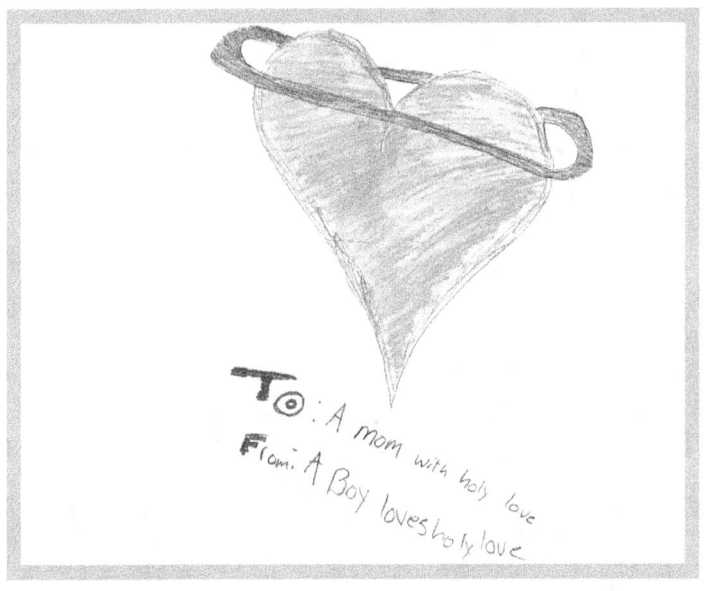

JOY ANNA

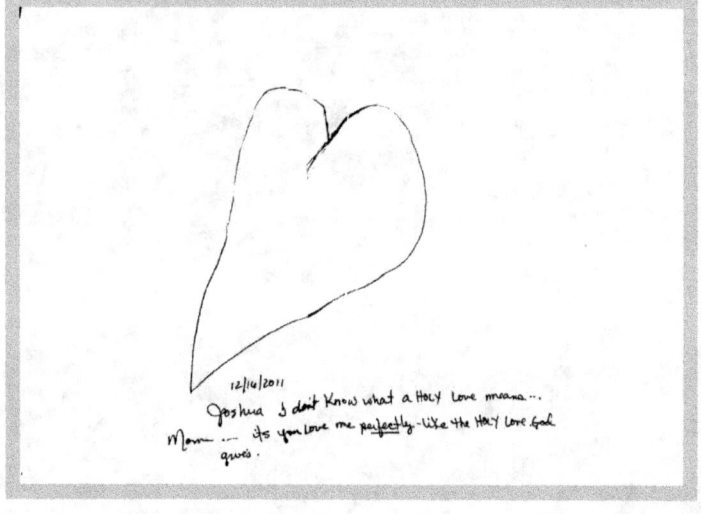

12/16/2011
Joshua: I don't know what a HOLY Love means...
Mom... it's you love me perfectly-like the HOLY Love God gives.

About the Author

I'm good at failing. I have failed at marriage. I have failed in business. I have failed at being a parent and my health has failed me. But failure is the key to success. With each failure I have gained insight and perspective not previously earned. Each failure has taught me to persevere.

My life has consisted of a series of events that gives me a perspective about what is really important. I hope that others can learn and be inspired by my failures.

I reside in a warm house, with a loving family, and a dog named Charlie.

facebook.com/AuthorJoyAnna
instagram.com/authorjoyanna

Also by Joy Anna

Coming Soon
What Is Charlie Doing?

Letter to the Reader

WHAT DID YOU THINK OF JUST JOSHIN' YA?

First of all, thank you for purchasing this book Just Joshin' Ya. I know you could have picked any number of books to read, but you picked this book, and for that, I am extremely grateful.

I hope that it added humor, value, and quality to your everyday life. If so, it would be really nice to share this book with your friends and family by posting to Facebook and Twitter.

If you enjoyed this book and found some benefit in reading it, I'd like to hear from you and hope that you could take some time to post a review on Amazon and/or Goodreads. Your feedback and support will help me to greatly improve my writing craft for future projects.

You can follow this link to my website Jo.Yanna.me.

Warmest Regards,

Joyanna Diaz

Joyanna "Joy" Diaz

www.ingramcontent.com/pod-product-compliance
Lightning Source LLC
Chambersburg PA
CBHW050335120526
44592CB00014B/2187